BUILDING A
RESILIENT
LIFE

HOW ADVERSITY AWAKENS
STRENGTH, HOPE, AND MEANING

BIBLE STUDY GUIDE

FIVE SESSIONS

REBEKAH LYONS

WITH KEVIN AND SHERRY HARNEY

HarperChristian
Resources

Building a Resilient Life Study Guide

© 2023 by Rebekah Lyons

Requests for information should be addressed to:
HarperChristian Resources, 3900 Sparks Dr. SE, Grand Rapids, Michigan 49546

ISBN 978-0-310-14932-3 (softcover)
ISBN 978-0-310-14933-0 (ebook)

Author is represented by Meredith Brock at The Brock Agency.

First Printing April 2023 / Printed in the United States of America

---

23 24 25 26 27 28 29 30 31 32 /TRM/ 15 14 13 12 11 10 9 8 7 6 5 4 3 2 1

CONTENTS

STORMS

Every generation faces storms. No family moves through time untouched by the tragedies of life. Each person born on this planet is confronted by pain, brokenness, and evil. Since the forbidden fruit was eaten and sin came crashing into paradise, the storms of our common humanity rage.

Along with the reality of cosmic brokenness, we also experience joy, we see beauty, and we have seasons of indescribable delight. Life is a mixed bag and we rarely know what is just around the corner. If we are going to press forward with resilient hearts and stability in the storms, there are God-given guidelines to help us along. No matter what comes our way, there is hope in Jesus and strength to hang in there and press through.

This generation has been no exception. A new virus made its way around the world and things changed in ways no one was prepared for. Through it all we adapted, resilient as we were. The country of Ukraine was invaded and images of war hit devices carried in the pockets and purses of people all over the globe. Gas prices boomed. Supply chain issues seemed to impact the availability of almost everything. Inflation became a common word and reality. Mortgage rates moved up drastically. The list could go on and on but you have lived these realities. These are the sort of things that live in the consciousness of our generation and they can ignite fear, worry, anxiety, and depression.

This is not to say that everything is terrible and without hope. Every sunrise is still beautiful, each act of kindness still amazing, the laughter of a child still brings a smile to our face. All of life is worth grasping and loving. But it does also feel as though things are somehow less forgiving, somehow more fragile, somehow more precarious.

Since you're walking through this study guide, I have a strong hunch you're looking for answers in this reality we all face together. You may have found yourself asking:

Why do I feel so fragile?

Should I give up or stay the course?

Will I recover passion and meaning?

Can I become resilient against the never-ending storms of life?

How do I know you're asking these questions? Because I'm asking them, too. Most of us are.

My prayer is that this five-session study will help us discover some meaningful and helpful answers to these questions.

With you on the journey,

Rebekah

OF NOTE

The study introduction and quotations interspersed throughout this study guide are excerpts from the book *Building a Resilient Life* and the video curriculum of the same name by Rebekah Lyons. All other resources, including the session introductions, small-group questions, prayer direction, and between-sessions materials have been written by Kevin and Sherry Harney in collaboration with Rebekah Lyons.

NAME THE PAIN

Pain is always pounding on the door of our lives and seeking to knock us down. This should not surprise us. The first step in growing resilient is acknowledging our pain, naming it, and taking wise steps to face it head-on.

INTRODUCTION

Group leader, read the introduction to the group before showing the video for this session.

Erika's GPA is over 4.2. With regular Advanced Placement classes, she is positioning herself to graduate and enroll in whatever college she chooses. She plays two sports and writes for the school newspaper. Her friends like her, and she has a vibrant social life—when she can make the time. To all outside observers, Erika appears to be happy and well-adjusted, living the dream! What no one knows is how she feels anytime she looks in the mirror (if she can force herself to do it). She avoids eating because she thinks she is overweight. Erika is pretty, athletic, and thin, but she carries the pain of self-hatred and sees herself as profoundly unattractive.

Char has two healthy and active children. Every Sunday, she arrives to church early, and her kids always look well-dressed and well-adjusted. Her husband, Ken, works on weekends, but Char tells everyone he says hi and wishes he could be there. Her smile lights up a room and her care for others is an example of the love and compassion of Jesus. To all casual onlookers, Char seems to have an ideal life and family. What no one knows is that Char and Ken barely speak to each other, and when they do, the sparks always seem to fly. Ken does not actually work on Sundays, but his drinking on Saturday nights makes it almost impossible for him to get up and make it to church.

Harold is retired, plays a lot of golf, and volunteers in his community whenever he can. He is gregarious and outgoing, and he tends to be the life of the party. When he's with others, Harold seems to be doing great. When he goes into his condo and closes the door, his smile fades quickly. It has been ten months and three days since Harold buried his wife, Sue, and it is rare for his friends to ask about her anymore. The world seems to have moved on, but after forty-eight years of marriage, a piece of Harold has died, and he simply has no idea how to fill the chasm in his heart and life.

In the worst of grief God promises to hold us, keep us, carry us, and never leave or forsake us.

TALK ABOUT IT

Share a time when you were walking through loss or pain and the people around you had no idea what you were really facing day after day.

_____

_____

_____

_____

_____

_____

_____

_____

_____

_____

_____

TEACHING NOTES

FROM VIDEO SESSION 1

As you watch the teaching segment for this session, use the following outline to record anything that stands out to you.

Why write a study on the topic of resilience?

Adversity can strengthen us or crush us ... What will it be?

Adversity Wakens the heart

_____

Adversity awakens us to what we are made of, what
we care about, and what is worth fighting for.

_____

God shows up in times of adversity and pain ... Always

Adversity awakens us to a choice ... What will you choose?

Choose hope

The ambiguity of loss

Resilience Defined: 2 Corinthians 3:17–4:18

Resilience is:	Resilience is not:
- *Remembering Gods promises*	*Giving up*
- *Perserverence*	
« *When it's time to stop knaes*	

How Jesus modeled resilience . . . Hebrews 12:1–3

Plowed thru

It is tempting to try to move past pain as quickly as possible.

Death of a dream . . . A liturgy by Douglas McKelvey

Name the Pain

    1. Understand Shame

    1. Unfiltered Confession

    1. Invite Others In

GROUP DISCUSSION

1. Consistently facing moderate and predictable stress and challenges in life can actually strengthen us and make us more capable of facing bigger and more complex challenges. Discuss how you have experienced this truth in some areas of your life.

2. *Group leader, look up and read aloud each passage or invite a volunteer to do so:* **Hebrews 12:1–3.**

   What are some things we are called to do in this passage and how might doing them help us grow more resilient?

   _____

   What if we embraced our struggles to develop the strength of resilience?

   _____

3. *Group leader, look up and read aloud each passage or invite a volunteer to do so:* **2 Corinthians 4:7–10.**

   How is this passage both deeply honest about pain and profoundly encouraging in the hope it brings? Why would this be a good passage to read and reflect on when you are walking through times of loss, struggle, and pain?

4. *Group leader, look up and read aloud each passage or invite a volunteer to do so:* **2 Corinthians 4:16–18.**

   What are some ways we can fix our eyes and hearts on the eternal glory God has for us? How can this help us grow more resilient and hopeful in the midst of the hard seasons we will all face?

5. *Group leader, look up and read aloud each passage or invite a volunteer to do so:* **Romans 8:1–4.**

   What are some ways our culture and the enemy of our souls try to heap shame on us? How does the truth revealed in the Bible combat the deceitful power of shame?

6. *Group leader, look up and read aloud each passage or invite a volunteer to do so:* **Psalm 18:3–6, 16–19.**

   In this psalm of David, we hear echoes of both honest confession and deep hope. How can unfiltered confession to God of how we feel, where we are spiritually, and our own struggles help us press on and follow God, even in profoundly painful times?

7. We live in a culture that can isolate us and cut us off from others. How can you invite other Christians into your life at a level that will allow them to encourage, support, and help you when you're facing difficult times? How can your group members pray for you and encourage you in an area of pain you are facing today?

We were never meant to walk this road alone.

CLOSING PRAYER

Spend time in your group praying together. The group leader may pray over the group or ask for volunteers. Below are some suggested prayer prompts:

- Acknowledge to God that you need to grow in resilience and that you invite him to deepen this desire in you over the upcoming weeks as you learn in community with your group members.

- Invite God to enter your places of pain, loss, and struggle.

- Pray for courage to open your heart and life to God and your group members over the coming sessions as you learn about resiliency together.

- Thank Jesus for being a powerful model of a resilient life while he walked on this earth.

- Silently talk with God about whatever you may need to confess to him as you begin this journey.

_____

We are truly resilient when we bring everything to Christ weathered and worn and allow ourselves to be filled and remade in the original shape of our Creator.

_____

WRAP-UP

Group leader, read the following wrap-up as you conclude your group session:

Resiliency is a gift that most of us never knew we needed. But as you walked through this session, there's a good chance you discovered that your heart is longing for God to grow this valuable trait in you. The first step is to name our pain. When we stop running, denying, and ignoring the struggles of life, we can turn and face them side by side with Jesus. When we invite others to stand with us, we experience the fortification of Christian community that God delights to give. Commit to stepping into this journey with a hope-filled heart and anticipation of the great things God wants to do in you.

_____

Life is less about mastery and more about the unfolding of faith and the process of being made new.

_____

BETWEEN SESSIONS

Make time in three days of the upcoming week to go deeper into **Building a Resilient Life** by using the resources provided here in your study guide. If you do these exercises slowly and reflectively each day, it should take about 20–30 minutes.

PERSONAL STUDY

NAME THE PAIN

Day 1

Take time to begin learning and meditating on this week's memory verse. Reflect on how your outlook on life could change if your eyes were always fixed on Jesus.

Let us run with perseverance the race marked out for us, fixing our eyes on Jesus, the pioneer and perfecter of faith. For the joy set before him he endured the cross, scorning its shame, and sat down at the right hand of the throne of God. Consider him who endured such opposition from sinners, so that you will not grow weary and lose heart.

Hebrews 12:1–3

TRAINING YOUR EYES

Each time we walk through adversity, Jesus is right there, reminding us that he's not going anywhere, reminding us that we can build strength upon strength.

We are called to fix our eyes on Jesus. This doesn't mean we try to physically stare at him. Our Lord ascended to heaven and sits at the right hand of the Father. When Hebrews 12:1–3 invites us to "fix our eyes on Jesus" and "consider him," it is a call to train the eyes of our hearts to avoid all the distractions of life that scream for our attention. Instead, we are to consistently recognize that our Savior is with us—closer than we can even imagine. We should give him our attention and devotion. The call is to train our eyes to be highly attentive to our Savior's desires, ways, teachings, and will for our lives.

Make a list of the things in a normal day that tend to grab your attention. These can be negative things (anxious, ruminating thoughts), neutral things (food), or even positive things (the people in your life):

1. Cell phone - Instagram - world issues - corruption
2. Daily chores that need to get done
3. What's for dinner? 😕
4. Keeping schedules organized
5.
6.
7.

Reflect on how keeping your eyes on these things can distract you from focusing on what is ultimately more important (Jesus and his will for your life):

Not sure. I feel what I'm doing in life is His will - serving. When you're older the body is slower - everything takes longer.

Read the first chapter of John's gospel. Make a list of truths you learn about Jesus in this chapter (There are a lot of them!):

- Vs 1 "In the beginning - He was there
- Vs 3 "All things made by Him - active in creation
- Vs 9 Jesus was the true Light
- Vs 18 Only Jesus has seen God
- Vs 29 Jesus is the Lamb of God - takes away our sin
- Vs 49 You are Son of God - King of Israel - His diety

Make an effort to focus the eyes of your heart and mind on two or three of these truths over the next week. Every time you find your eyes wandering, turn your attention to these biblical messages about who Jesus is and how he is alive and at work in the world and in your life.

Resliene
To bend & not break

Day 2

Continue memorizing and meditating on this week's verse. Think about what Jesus endured for you and be in awe of the spiritual reality that he was filled with joy as he went to the cross because he knew the end result—giving you the priceless gift of entering into a relationship with him.

Let us run with perseverance the race marked out for us, fixing our eyes on Jesus, the pioneer and perfecter of faith. For the joy set before him he endured the cross, scorning its shame, and sat down at the right hand of the throne of God. Consider him who endured such opposition from sinners, so that you will not grow weary and lose heart.

Hebrews 12:1–3

LESSONS ON RESILIENCY

Resilience is faithful perseverance.

Take time to dig into **2 Corinthians 3:17–4:18**. Look for three specific truths that come through in this passage.

1. **Underline:** As you first read this passage, look for what you can learn about Jesus and underline each truth in the lesson.

2. **Circle:** As you read through a second time, circle each lesson you learn about the pain and struggles that faithful followers of Jesus can face as they walk through life.

3. **Highlight:** As you read this passage a third time, use a highlighter and mark the portions of this passage that give you hope, confidence, or a vision of how God will strengthen you and lead you through the painful times you will face.

> Now the Lord is the Spirit, and where the Spirit of the Lord is, there is freedom. And we all, who with unveiled faces contemplate the Lord's glory, are being transformed into his image with ever-increasing glory, which comes from the Lord, who is the Spirit.
>
> Therefore, since through God's mercy we have this ministry, we do not lose heart. Rather, we have renounced secret and shameful ways; we do not use deception, nor do we distort the word of God. On the contrary, by setting forth the truth plainly we commend ourselves to everyone's conscience in the sight of God. And even if our gospel is veiled, it is veiled to those who are perishing. The god of this age has blinded the minds of unbelievers, so that they cannot see the light of the gospel that displays the glory of Christ, who is the image of God. For what we preach is not ourselves, but Jesus Christ as Lord, and ourselves as your servants for Jesus' sake. For God, who said, "Let light shine out of darkness," made his light shine in our hearts to give us the light of the knowledge of God's glory displayed in the face of Christ.
>
> But we have this treasure in jars of clay to show that this all-surpassing power is from God and not from us. We are hard pressed on every side, but not crushed; perplexed, but not in despair; persecuted, but not abandoned; struck down, but not destroyed. We always carry around in our body the death of Jesus, so that the life of Jesus may also be revealed in our body.

For we who are alive are always being given over to death for Jesus' sake, so that his life may also be revealed in our mortal body. So then, death is at work in us, but life is at work in you.

It is written: "I believed; therefore I have spoken." Since we have that same spirit of faith, we also believe and therefore speak, because we know that the one who raised the Lord Jesus from the dead will also raise us with Jesus and present us with you to himself. All this is for your benefit, so that the grace that is reaching more and more people may cause thanksgiving to overflow to the glory of God.

Therefore we do not lose heart. Though outwardly we are wasting away, yet inwardly we are being renewed day by day. For our light and momentary troubles are achieving for us an eternal glory that far outweighs them all. So we fix our eyes not on what is seen, but on what is unseen, since what is seen is temporary, but what is unseen is eternal.

In your own words, write down three or four lessons you learn from this passage about how God brings resiliency to those who follow him and hold on to Jesus:

1. We do not loose heart
2. We are being renewed day by day
3. Our troubles are momentary
4. What is unseen is eternal

Ask the Holy Spirit to bring these truths to your heart as you walk through the upcoming week.

Day 3

Conclude your time learning and meditating on this week's passage. Ask Jesus to help you not grow weary or lose heart but become more resilient as you face the very real challenges of this life.

Let us run with perseverance the race marked out for us, fixing our eyes on Jesus, the pioneer and perfecter of faith. For the joy set before him he endured the cross, scorning its shame, and sat down at the right hand of the throne of God. Consider him who endured such opposition from sinners, so that you will not grow weary and lose heart.

Hebrews 12:1–3

THE BEAUTY OF CONFESSION AND REPENTANCE

When we confess our hidden sins (and sometimes they are hidden even from us), God is always ready to remind us of his staggering forgiveness. When we turn away from our actions and attitudes of sin (repent), a fresh wind of God's presence and grace blows through the hallways of our lives. Beauty and grace fill our lives when we humbly seek God and place our brokenness at his feet.

Resilience is **not** naive optimism.

Take some time to quietly reflect on the past week. What are some places where you were enticed to sin in thoughts, attitudes, or actions?

-
-
-
-
-

Read **1 John 1:9–10** slowly and confidently. You may even want to read it out loud a few times. You could try personalizing this passage: "If I confess my sins …"

If we confess our sins, he is faithful and just and will forgive us our sins and purify us from all unrighteousness. If we claim we have not sinned, we make him out to be a liar and his word is not in us.

Do all you can to find a quiet and private place where you can kneel (if you are able) and spend time placing your sins before Jesus, confessing them, and telling him you are truly sorry. Then commit to turn, change, stop, and repent. Ask for the power of the Holy Spirit to strengthen you to keep walking away from sin and toward Jesus.

Optional

RECOMMENDED READING

As you reflect on what God is teaching you through this session, you may want to read chapters 4–6 of Rebekah's book *Building a Resilient Life*.

SHIFT THE NARRATIVE

The world is filled with all sorts of lies and too often, we buy in! The enemy of our soul is called "the father of lies," and Jesus was clear that Satan's native language is deceit. If we are going to grow in resiliency, we need to identify the lies we believe, reject them, and embrace the truth.

INTRODUCTION

Group leader, read the introduction to the group before showing the video for this session.

When we live in this world, we breathe the air of false narratives. Some seem benign, and others deadly. All of them should be confronted by the One whose name is "Truth." Jesus is not only the **Way** and the **Life**; He is also the **Truth** (John 14:6). When we know the truth, we can question false narratives and reject them.

In 1971, the Coca-Cola company released a commercial with young people from around the world singing on a hilltop. They declared, with smiling faces and beautiful voices, "I'd like to teach the world to sing in perfect harmony!" As the camera moves across this sea of joy-filled peace seekers, we discover that one of the keys to the world harmony they desire is giving everyone a bottle filled with carbonated sugar water. You don't have to dig very deep to find the false narrative in this advertising strategy.

Throughout the history of the church, there have been examples of false narratives. For nearly five hundred years, from around 1095 to 1567, people could buy an indulgence from the church to get rid of past sins. The Bible is clear that forgiveness is found in Jesus' sacrifice and faith in him alone. But this did not stop church leaders from raising lots of money by selling documents that assured people that their past wrongs were washed away by their "donation" to the church. Even "religious" people are tempted to create false narratives if it increases their bottom lines.

In a world filled with false narratives and deceptive people, Christians need to look to the Bible for truth and learn to identify when something is false and needs to be replaced by the truth.

_____

Faith trusts what Jesus declares is true.

_____

TALK ABOUT IT

Share a false narrative you have seen or heard and explain how knowing the truth helped you identify the false narrative and resist it.

_____

_____

_____

_____

_____

_____

_____

_____

_____

_____

_____

_____

_____

TEACHING NOTES
FROM VIDEO SESSION 2

As you watch the teaching segment for this session, use the following outline to record anything that stands out to you.

Stuck in a loop . . . The danger of falling for a lie

_____

_____

When the pressure goes up and our fuel tank runs low

_____

_____

_____

We were created not to survive but to overcome.

_____

The spiral of shame

_____

_____

The power of confession . . . A fresh perspective

_____

_____

_____

Confession is the gateway to healing from shame.

_____

The truth of God's Word . . . Reshaping our thinking

We are adopted by God.

We are heirs of the throne.

We are sons and daughters of the King.

God's love knows no bounds.

Our good works can't increase God's love for us.

Digging into God's Word . . . How the truth sets us free

1. Prepare in advance

2. Routines for resilience

Withhold nothing from God

GROUP DISCUSSION

1. Rebekah began the video session by describing how she got stuck in a loop of believing the false narrative that she needed the approval of others rather than being content to live a life that pleases God. Why is believing the false narrative that you have to please every person you encounter so dangerous? What are some consequences we might face if we let this narrative run wild in our hearts and direct our daily decisions?

_____

When you work for an audience of one, you always know that you count.

_____

2. *Group leader, look up and read aloud the following passage or invite a volunteer to do so:* **Matthew 11:28–30**.

   These words of Jesus can revolutionize your life! What is the heartbeat of Jesus' message in this passage? How might your life change if you were to truly accept and embrace this narrative rather than the world's call to perform and constantly produce?

3. How has the false narrative of shame impacted your life in the past or present? What are signs and signals that we are being driven by shame?

4. *Group leader, look up and read aloud the following passage or invite a volunteer to do so:* **Romans 10:8–10**.

One aspect of confession is telling God we are sorry for our sins and wrong thoughts and actions. Another expression of confession is boldly declaring what we know to be true. What is being confessed in this passage and why is it so central to the Christian faith? What are some biblical truths that will help drive away shame if we confess them with consistent confidence?

_____

Confession can also mean declaring something emphatically such as our faith.

_____

5. Tell about your experience with the Bible, going back to your earliest recollections (for some this will be childhood, for others it will be the teen years, and, for some it will be recent times). What role does the Bible play in this season of your life?

6. What practices of reading the Bible (or listening to it) have you found helpful as you infuse truth into your mind and heart? How can your group members pray for you, cheer you on, and partner with you in your practices of digging deeply into the Scriptures and putting into practice what the Bible teaches?

7. Group leader, look up and read aloud the following passage or invite a volunteer to do so. Be sure to read it slowly and reflectively: **Psalm 23**.

What truths in this psalm can lift up your soul and fortify your trust in the Good Shepherd? How might meditating on these truths help you reject some of this world's false narratives?

_____

We grow in faith before we need it.

_____

CLOSING PRAYER

Spend time in your group praying together. The group leader may pray over the group or ask for volunteers. Below are some suggested prayer prompts:

- Confess where false narratives, cultural lies, and deceptions of the enemy have captured your heart and adversely impacted your life.

- Ask Jesus to give you a deep confidence that what he has for you is not meant to be a burden that weighs you down but a calling that fits just who he has made you to be.

- Offer prayers that declare the truth of God revealed in the Scriptures. Declare these to God and all of heaven as a bold confession that you believe and embrace God's truth!

- Ask the Holy Spirit to grow your love for the Bible and to empower you to feast on God's truth with ever-increasing hunger.

- If you have a Bible verse or brief passage of Scripture you love that captures a powerful truth, look it up, read it out loud, and pray that each member of your group will walk in this truth and allow it to shift the narrative of his or her life.

The act of surrender, of naming our pain, of bringing our suffering into the light, is meaningless without the perspective of Christ as our living hope.

WRAP-UP

Group leader, read the following wrap-up as you conclude your group session:

The world will never stop spewing lies and crafting ever-increasing false narratives. This is an ongoing battle, and the enemy of our soul is really good at telling lies. We need to identify the deceitful messages of the enemy, name them, reject them, and replace them with God's truth. As we do that, we will grow resilient and experience ever-increasing joy and peace.

———————

Jesus doesn't say you can be or may be or will be free; he says you are free.

———————

BETWEEN SESSIONS

Make time in three days of the upcoming week to go deeper into **Building a Resilient Life** by using the resources provided here in your study guide. If you do these exercises slowly and reflectively each day, it should take about 20–30 minutes.

PERSONAL STUDY

SHIFT THE NARRATIVE

Day 1

Take time to begin learning and meditating on this week's memory verse. Reflect on Jesus' declaration that there is truth. In our relativistic world, it is important for us to believe our Savior's divine authority on this topic.

*Then you will know the truth, and
the truth will set you free.*

John 8:32

A BIGGER UNDERSTANDING OF CONFESSION

———————

Confession begins with repentance
and ends with declaration.

———————

One important aspect of confession that often gets missed is boldly declaring what we know to be true from the pages of the Bible. When we confess, over and over, the piercing truth that God has revealed, we fortify ourselves against the false narratives of our culture and the spiritual deceit of the enemy. Take time to dig deeply into these four truths so that you can learn to confess them and lock them in your heart.

KEY PASSAGE #1 (write it in the space below)**: Romans 8:14–17**

What truth is God teaching you in this passage?

What lies and false narratives can this truth help you resist?

Write this truth as a personal confession.

Pause right now and lift up this confession as a bold declaration of prayer!

KEY PASSAGE #2 (write it in the space below): **Ephesians 2:8–10**

_____

_____

_____

_____

————————

There's a fine line we cross where our
work becomes our worth.

————————

What truth is God teaching you in this passage?

_____

_____

What lies and false narratives can this truth help you resist?

_____

_____

_____

_____

Write this truth as a personal confession.

_____

_____

_____

Pause right now and lift up this confession as a bold declaration of prayer!

KEY PASSAGE #3 (write it in the space below): **1 John 4:2–4**

_____

_____

_____

_____

What truth is God teaching you in this passage?

_____

_____

_____

What lies and false narratives can this truth help you resist?

_____

_____

_____

_____

_____

_____

_____

_____

Write this truth as a personal confession.

_____

_____

_____

_____

Pause right now and lift up this confession as a bold declaration of prayer!

KEY PASSAGE #4 (write it in the space below): **Titus 3:4–8**

_____

_____

_____

_____

What truth is God teaching you in this passage?

_____

_____

What lies and false narratives can this truth help you resist?

_____

_____

_____

_____

_____

Write this truth as a personal confession.

_____

_____

_____

Pause right now and lift up this confession as a bold declaration of prayer!

Day 2

Continue memorizing and meditating on this week's verse. Not only is there truth, but we can know the truth! God's truth is not cryptic, hidden, or out of our reach. Our Savior was clear that there is truth and that we can know it. This is a hope-filled reality!

Then you will know the truth, and
the truth will set you free.

John 8:32

MY FALSE NARRATIVES

If we are going to be people of resilience, it's important to recognize the narratives we tell ourselves, particularly those that are untrue.

We all have false narratives we can slip into if we are not aware and careful. We can slip into these narratives—like ruts in a road—and hardly notice we are doing it. Maybe our family history has been passed on to us with both good and bad narratives we've embraced. Perhaps the narratives are cultural norms we've barely noticed but have adopted as our own. No matter where these false narratives originate, it is essential to identify them and let the truth of Scripture shift our thinking and redefine the narratives that guide our lives.

Take time to prayerfully **identify three false narratives** that run freely through the hallways of your mind and heart. You did not invite them in, but they've taken up residency and refuse to leave on their own. Name them and write them down in the spaces below:

False Narrative 1:

_____

_____

_____

False Narrative 2:

_____

_____

_____

False Narrative 3:

_____

_____

_____

Write down **two or three possible harmful consequences** if you were to let each of these false narratives continue to reside in your mind and life:

Consequences if I let False Narrative 1 continue to grow in me:

- _____

- _____

- _____

Consequences if I let False Narrative 2 keep living in my mind and heart:

🌀 _____

🌀 _____

🌀 _____

Consequences if I let False Narrative 3 continue to live in me:

🌀 _____

🌀 _____

🌀 _____

Reflect and write down **one specific truth** you can meditate on or **action you can take** that will flip the script and shift each one of these narratives.

A truth or action that will battle back against False Narrative 1:

_____

_____

A truth or action that will bring truth and shift False Narrative 2:

_____

_____

A truth or action that will neutralize False Narrative 3:

_____

_____

Day 3

As you conclude your week of learning and meditating on this verse, be confident that there is truth, rejoice that you can know God's truth, and then delight in the promise that following God's truth leads to freedom. Walk in that knowledge and be assured that knowing the truth and living in it leads to a resilient life.

> *Then you will know the truth, and*
> *the truth will set you free.*
>
> **John 8:32**

LEARNING FROM THE SHEPHERD

The truth of God's Word is the greatest antidote to the poison of false narratives. Take time to read, reflect on, and learn from the most famous of all 150 psalms. As you read this beautiful "Shepherd Psalm," you will lock powerful truths into your heart.

As you read and reflect:

- **Underline** any truths you learn about God, the Good Shepherd of your soul.

- **Circle** any truths you learn about yourself.

> The Lord *is my shepherd, I lack nothing.*
> *He makes me lie down in green pastures,*
> *he leads me beside quiet waters,*
> *he refreshes my soul.*
>
> *He guides me along the right paths*
> *for his name's sake.*

Even though I walk
   through the darkest valley,

I will fear no evil,
   for you are with me;
your rod and your staff,
   they comfort me.

You prepare a table before me
   in the presence of my enemies.
You anoint my head with oil;
   my cup overflows.

Surely your goodness and love will follow me
   all the days of my life,
and I will dwell in the house of the LORD
   forever. (Psalm 23)

Write down the three most impactful truths you learn about God your Shepherd:

🔖 _____

🔖 _____

🔖 _____

Write down the three most impactful truths you learn about yourself, a sheep loved by God:

🔖 _____

🔖 _____

🔖 _____

Spend a few quiet moments thanking God for who he is and who you are because of his grace and love.

RECOMMENDED READING

As you reflect on what God is teaching you through this session, you may want to read chapters 7–9 of Rebekah's book *Building a Resilient Life*.

EMBRACE ADVERSITY

Are you ready for a radically countercultural shock? The best way to overcome pain, discomfort, anxiety, and fear is to face it and move toward it—hand in hand with Jesus. When we embrace adversity rather than run from it, we will grow more and more resilient.

INTRODUCTION

Group leader, read the introduction to the group before showing the video for this session.

Many things in life make perfect sense. If you touch a sizzling hot pan, you reflexively pull your hand back. That is exactly the right response. When we look at our finances and realize we're running low on spendable cash, we tighten the belt and buy less. To do otherwise would be foolish. When the red light on our dashboard tells us we are about to run out of gas, to ignore it would be irresponsible. We look for the next gas station (unless we're a thrill seeker or enjoy long walks on the side of the road).

In most situations we face, there is a logical and sensible way to respond. But in some situations, the best response is counterintuitive. The healthy or wise way to act seems to go against our natural instincts or what we think is just plain common sense. Here are some examples of this reality:

- Learning to say no more effectively can free you to say yes more often.

- The more you try to control another person or force them to like you, the more likely they are to pull away from you.

- The best way to have free time in your schedule and space to really relax is to plan ahead and structure your life.

- When you are really tired and don't want to exercise, one thing that can invigorate your energy level is being active and exercising.

- When you try to make everyone happy, you often make no one happy.

- Being willing to fail can lead to great success over time.

You get the idea. Sometimes things that don't make sense are the best way forward.

This is absolutely true when it comes to overcoming adversity, anxiety, and fear. The natural response is to turn from it and run. Separation from stress feels like the best way to deal with it. The truth is actually counterintuitive. If we're going to move past our fears and the adversity that life brings our way, we need to embrace it wisely and consistently. Face it. Move toward it.

Adversity must be met with an equal opposite and more powerful reaction. Instead of avoiding it, we must confront it.

TALK ABOUT IT

Share a lesson you learned that was counterintuitive. The right way forward did not look like the best way—until you moved forward.

_____

_____

_____

_____

_____

_____

_____

_____

_____

TEACHING NOTES
FROM SESSION 3

As you watch the teaching segment for this session, use the following outline to record anything that stands out to you.

Resilience grows as we embrace adversity . . . So face it boldly with Jesus

_____

When we encounter adversity, we face a challenge that requires a decision. Will we run and hide, or will we embrace and overcome?

_____

A real-life story . . . When fear and panic descend

Don't run away . . . Meditate (train your mind)

Good things can happen when we turn toward our pain

We identify things that are not well.

We take a closer look at our lives.

We can affirm our dependence on Jesus.

We learn the value of meditating on Scripture.

We are moved to deeper places of bold prayer.

We often experience less pain over time.

Pain becomes purpose if you let it.

The value of meditating on God's Word

The danger of things being too easy

Our cultural hunger for "magic" and "superpowers"

_____

_____

Jesus did not choose the easy road

_____

_____

Easy does not connect us to others

_____

_____

Two kinds of adversity

_____

_____

The kind we can't control

_____

_____

The kind that is voluntary

_____

_____

The road to genuine Christian character . . . It demands endurance and resilience

_____

_____

_____

Character requires endurance. We have
to put the effort in to keep going.

_____

GROUP DISCUSSION

1. Share a time you moved toward your fear or some adversity. How did this lead to growth, a deeper faith, or an increased resiliency over time?

2. When you've faced times of adversity, stress, anxiety, pain, or loss, what tools have helped you press forward and make it through?

3. So many people today turn and run, shut down, or lock down at the first sign of adversity. What do they miss out on if they refuse to face their fears and move toward adversity? Why do you think God has designed us to grow the most when we face these hard times rather than avoid them?

4. When a person refuses to exercise because it is hard, the end result is that their muscles atrophy and become weaker. When we run away from hard experiences and painful circumstances, we actually become less resilient. Can you identify a life situation you know will be tough to face and even painful but you are confident God wants you to press into? How can your group members pray for you and encourage you as you face this challenge?

_____

> Just as physical exercise increases our body's capacity to handle and off-load stress, emotional and spiritual exercise does as well.

_____

5. *Group leader, look up and read aloud the following passage or invite a volunteer to do so:* **Joshua 1:7–9**.

Joshua was moving out from the shadow of Moses into the role of leading the nation of Israel. There were challenges ahead of him that we can hardly imagine. What did the Lord tell Joshua to do (there is a whole list)? How would each of these things equip Joshua to press past his fear and move boldly into God's plan for his life?

6. If you were to follow the wisdom that God spoke to Joshua in this critical and conflicted time of his life, how might these teachings and exhortations help you face the adversity and the challenging times you face?

7. *Group leader, look up and read aloud the following passage or invite a volunteer to do so:* **Psalm 3:1–6**.

In this psalm, it is clear that enemies and battles were on the horizon, right in front of David. The message was not that God would remove the adversity but that David would never be alone. What hope and encouragement do you receive as you read the words of David in this psalm? If God is truly the same yesterday, today, and forever, what do you learn about the God who is with you in your daily battles?

CLOSING PRAYER

Spend time in your group praying together. The group leader may pray over the group or ask for volunteers. Below are some suggested prayer prompts:

- Thank God that no matter what you face in this life, he will never leave you or forsake you. Lift up to him praise that he is a shield and deliverer!

- Acknowledge to God that in every moment of panic, pain, and adversity you have faced, he has been watching over you and using these trials to make you more of the person he wants you to be.

- Pray for courage to face the hard times that are ahead with bold faith as you walk toward things you are inclined to want to flee from.

- Thank God for the power of his Word and ask for discipline to meditate on his truth and follow the Bible's teaching as you face the hard times of life with courage, side by side with Jesus.

- Read **Psalm 3:1–6** as your own prayer and ask God to protect you and those you love.

_____

If life becomes too easy, we don't need other people and we don't need God. But neither of those things is true.

_____

WRAP-UP

Group leader, read the following wrap-up as you conclude your group session:

Our natural response when we see pain, adversity, and struggles on the horizons of our lives is to turn and run the other way. God calls us to embrace these moments in his strength and to press forward. As we do, we actually grow stronger and find greater peace and joy—even in the hard times.

———————

Let's commit to doing the countercultural thing, the hard thing. Let's push into embracing adversity.

———————

BETWEEN SESSIONS

Make time in three days of the upcoming week to go deeper into **Building a Resilient Life** by using the resources provided here in your study guide. If you do these exercises slowly and reflectively each day, it should take about 20–30 minutes.

PERSONAL STUDY

EMBRACE ADVERSITY

Day 1

Take time to begin learning and meditating on this week's memory verse. Ponder what it means to have "pure joy" when you face trying times.

Consider it pure joy, my brothers and sisters,
whenever you face trials of many kinds,
because you know that the testing of
your faith produces perseverance.

James 1:2–3

MARINATING IN THE SCRIPTURES

We become more like Christ and experience more of his character as we embrace the hard things and avoid complaining.

When food sits in a marinade for hours, the flavor soaks in. When we read biblical passages over and over and let them sink into our minds and souls, the message becomes part of us. Take time to read, reflect, pray over, and meditate on the following passages. You will quickly identify a couple of recurring truths and themes.

> *Consider it pure joy, my brothers and sisters, whenever you face trials of many kinds, because you know that the testing of your faith produces perseverance. Let perseverance finish its work so that you may be mature and complete, not lacking anything. If any of you lacks wisdom, you should ask God, who gives generously to all without finding fault, and it will be given to you. (James 1:2–5)*

May these words of my mouth and this meditation of my heart

be pleasing in your sight,

Lord, my Rock and my Redeemer. (Psalm 19:14)

"Be strong and very courageous. Be careful to obey all the law my servant Moses gave you; do not turn from it to the right or to the left, that you may be successful wherever you go. Keep this Book of the Law always on your lips; meditate on it day and night, so that you may be careful to do everything written in it. Then you will be prosperous and successful. Have I not commanded you? Be strong and courageous. Do not be afraid; do not be discouraged, for the Lord your God will be with you wherever you go." (Joshua 1:7–9)

The enemy pursues me,

he crushes me to the ground;

he makes me dwell in the darkness

like those long dead.

So my spirit grows faint within me;

my heart within me is dismayed.

I remember the days of long ago;

I mediate on all your works

and consider what your hands have done.

I spread out my hands to you;

I thirst for you like a parched land. (Psalm 143:3–6)

Hear this, all you peoples;

listen, all who live in this world,

both low and high,

rich and poor alike:

My mouth will speak words of wisdom;

the meditation of my heart will give you understanding.
(Psalm 49:1–3)

What are two or three themes in these passages that resonate in your soul:

- _____
- _____
- _____

Ask the Holy Spirit to bring these passages to mind as you seek to walk with Jesus, embrace adversity, and let the truth of Scripture dwell richly in your heart.

Day 2

Continue learning and meditating on this week's memory verse. As you think of the words "trials of many kinds," picture your trials and know that this passage applies to your life.

Consider it pure joy, my brothers and sisters, whenever you face trials of many kinds, because you know that the testing of your faith produces perseverance.

James 1:2–3

LEARNING FROM A MASTER

What if we become stronger, more whole, and more resilient when we face our challenges with a hopeful outlook?

When it comes to facing adversity, Job could teach a master class. The Old Testament book that bears his name has epic lessons for us to learn. Take time in the coming days to read some portions of Job and journal three things:

1. What kind of struggles and pain did Job face?

2. How did he face it? What were his disposition and attitude like?

3. What did he learn about God along the way?

Use the space provided (or your own journal if you keep one) to record your insights.

Take time to read **Job 1–3** and **38–42**.

_____

_____

_____

_____

_____

_____

_____

_____

_____

_____

_____

_____

_____

_____

_____

_____

_____

_____

_____

_____

Day 3

As you wrap up your time meditating on this week's memory verse, ask that God will grow perseverance and resiliency in you as you embrace the adversity you face.

Consider it pure joy, my brothers and sisters,
whenever you face trials of many kinds,
because you know that the testing of
your faith produces perseverance.

James 1:2-3

INVITE GOD IN

————————

Resilience is a muscle developed through
responding to adversity in the right ways.

————————

At the end of this session's video teaching, Rebekah urged you to invite God into your pain, anxiety, and adversity. At first glance, this may seem like a strange prayer: "God, please join me in the hardest times of life." But when you stop to think about it, what could be better? Hard times will come crashing into the lives of all of us. The wisest thing to do is proactively invite the God of the universe to travel these roads with us. It is actually the desire of his heart!

Take time to write out a prayer, a cry from your heart, a formal invitation to the God who made you and loves you. Let this be the moment you ask God to be with you in fresh, powerful, new ways—no matter what you are facing or will face in the journey ahead.

Use the space provided below to write your invitation:

_____

_____

_____

_____

_____

_____

_____

_____

_____

_____

_____

_____

_____

_____

RECOMMENDED READING

As you reflect on what God is teaching you through this session, you may want to read chapters 10–12 of Rebekah's book *Building a Resilient Life*.

MAKE MEANING

*Where do we find meaning in our confused and wandering world? We discover it when we look **outward** and see the glory and beauty of God's creation. We find meaning when we look **inward** at the calling and birthright gifts God placed in us from our mother's womb. Finally, we understand meaning when we look **upward** and see the face of our loving God.*

INTRODUCTION

Group leader, read the introduction to the group before showing the video for this session.

All throughout history, people have been seeking the meaning of life. This makes perfect sense! What could matter more than having a reason to live and finding meaning in the midst of life's confusion and pain? Something deep in the soul of every person hungers to know their purposes and reasons for living.

The quest for meaning has led people to isolate themselves in caves while they silently searched the darkness for a clue to why they are on this planet. People have climbed the highest mountains searching for an answer to life's riddles while their toes became numb from frostbite and their lungs screamed for oxygen. Others have experimented with hallucinogenic drugs in the heat of desert wastelands hoping to gain a glimpse of what really matters in life.

Countless people have looked for meaning in education and human knowledge. Boatloads of books are written and read. Classes are attended and digested. Studies are done and tuition bills are paid—sometimes for many years after the educational quest is completed and graduation hats have been propelled into the sky in celebration.

Religions and philosophies multiply with the years, and people keep searching for the meaning of existence. Sacrifices are placed on the altar, chants and mantras are repeated, penance is offered, and people seem to keep grasping for something that will satisfy them.

What if the search for meaning did not demand isolation in a cave, ever-increasing tuitions, or religious robes and liturgies? What if meaning could be as close as a walk along the beach or a span of time sitting quietly at home as we reflect on our own journey from our birth to today? What if we could make meaning by simply connecting with the God who made us and loves us?

Maybe meaning is closer than we think.

God wants to reawaken meaning in your life.

TALK ABOUT IT

How have you seen people (including yourself) search for meaning in complex and costly ways?

_____

_____

_____

_____

_____

Busyness is the saboteur of discovering and making meaning.

TEACHING NOTES

FROM VIDEO SESSION 4

As you watch the teaching segment for this session, use the following outline to record anything that stands out to you.

Creation reveals meaning . . . How beauty, God's presence, and truth are seen in the world around us

_____

_____

Made in the image of God . . . We were designed to create and be creative

_____

_____

————————

This compulsion to create is innate in all of us, the *imago dei* of our Creator on display in our lives.

————————

Making meaning

_____

_____

What do you really want? ... These things and so much more

_____

_____

To love and be loved

_____

_____

Biblical justice

Meaningful labor

Adventure

True connection with God

Learn to recognize beauty . . . It is all around us

God's beauty is in us

God's calling and birthright gifts . . . These are natural and effortless but still need to be nurtured

Calling always begins with a caller.

When there is no meaning . . . We wander and squander

_____

_____

Wake up to meaning . . . Jump in and enjoy the adventure

_____

_____

——————————

We are all born to make meaning.

——————————

GROUP DISCUSSION

1. *Group leader, look up and read aloud the following passage or invite a volunteer to do so:* **Psalm 8:1–4**.

   Can you identify a place in God's creation where you feel connected to him and sense his presence, and how does this place speak to you about God's meaning for your life?

   _____

   > Beauty begins in the beholding, and
   > the beholding propels action.

   _____

2. *Group leader, look up and read aloud the following passages or invite a volunteer to do so:* **Psalm 139:1–6, 13–18**.

   What do you learn about God in this psalm, and what do you learn about yourself? How do these truths speak to you about your life's meaning?

3. When we ponder the question "What do I want?" it's easy to give quick and shallow answers. Take a moment to reflect on this question prayerfully and thoughtfully: What do you really want in this life? What really matters and adds meaning to life? Use the space below to write down three things that you really long for in your deepest heart and soul:

   🌀 _____

   🌀 _____

   🌀 _____

   Share **one** of these with your group and explain why it is so important to you.

4. Tell about a time you received or experienced something that mattered deeply to you. How did this moment help make sense of things and add meaning to your life?

5. Think back to your childhood and reflect on what you loved, what came naturally, what you gravitated toward. If you're still doing one of these things, share about it and how it brings meaning to your life and connects you to God. If you're no longer doing one of these things, tell about when you stopped and reflect on whether it would be good for your soul to reengage in this activity.

Because you are made in God's image, when you create, you are infused with his imagination to set the world right.

----

6. Rebekah talks about how acting on our birthright gifts comes naturally and is also nurtured. Growing these gifts is both **effortless** and **cultivated**. While this statement may seem paradoxical, both sides of this reality are important. Talk about one of your talents or gifts, describing how it comes naturally from the Lord but also how you can develop, sharpen, and nurture it.

7. What is a gift or talent that God has placed in you—one you believe needs to be awakened and rekindled? Can you identify a next step you can take to reclaim meaning in your life by embracing once again this gifting from God? How can your group members support you, pray for you, and cheer you on as you step back into this place of meaning and purpose?

Encountering beauty and making good things can help us cultivate purpose and create meaning.

CLOSING PRAYER

Spend time in your group praying together. The group leader may pray over the group or ask for volunteers. Below are some suggested prayer prompts:

- Think about a place in creation that you love and that connects you to God. Offer a prayer of praise to God for using his amazing creative power to make this place.

- Psalm 139 reminds us that God personally and intimately crafted us in our mother's womb. Thank God for the way he has made you and acknowledge the wonder of his creativity.

- Ask God to grow in you the longings and desires that most glorify him.

- Offer back to God the birthright gifts he has placed in you. Pray for courage and faithfulness as you use them for his glory.

- Pray for group members who have shared that they want to reignite one of their talents or birthright gifts. Ask for God to infuse them with hope, excitement, and the power they need to embrace this gift once again.

God knit us with intention in our mother's womb.
He formed us from dust, and as image bearers,
we are invited to the same kind of creativity as
we cultivate purpose and seek meaning.

WRAP-UP

Group leader, read the following wrap-up as you conclude your group session:

You don't have to climb Mount Everest or get a master's degree to find the meaning God has for your life. Just open your eyes and drink in the beauty of his creation. Look deep into your own heart and soul—examine your past and reflect on your dreams for the future—and see what God has placed in you. Turn your eyes and heart to heaven and look to the God who loves you, calls you, pours out his gifts on you, and has amazing plans for your life. The key is not making your own meaning; it is discovering God's meaning for you and following his leading each and every day.

———————————

Beauty is the antidote to scarcity.
When we fear, we see lack.

———————————

BETWEEN SESSIONS

Make time in three days of the upcoming week to go deeper into **Building a Resilient Life** by using the resources provided here in your study guide. If you do these exercises slowly and reflectively each day, it should take about 20–30 minutes.

PERSONAL STUDY

MAKE MEANING

Day 1

Take time to begin learning and meditating on this week's memory verse. Reflect on how the creation you see each day reflects the beauty and character of the Creator.

The heavens declare the glory of God; the
skies proclaim the work of his hands.

Psalm 19:1

NOTICING AND CELEBRATING CREATION

_____

When we recognize beauty, we encounter the divine.

_____

Take time in the upcoming week to intentionally drink in the beauty and glory of God's creation. Use the space below to record the ways you see God's handiwork and sense his presence, as well as the things you are learning about his character.

Begin by looking outside. If you find yourself near mountains, a beach, a nice park, a forest preserve, take a good thirty minutes to walk around or sit in this place. Look closely. Listen. Smell. Feel the glory of God. Then write down a few things you experienced:

How did I experience the creative beauty of God?

_____

_____

_____

_____

What did I learn about the person and character of God?

_____

_____

_____

_____

How did I feel wonder and awe as I focused on what God has made?

_____

_____

_____

_____

Next, take a look a little closer to home. Focus on yourself. Your body, heart, mind, soul—all that makes you who you are. This exercise may stretch you because many of us can see God more in a kitten or a sunset than in ourselves. But according to the opening chapters of the book of Genesis, human beings are the pinnacle of God's creation, and we reflect his presence and glory more than anything else. Use the space below to thoughtfully and honestly record some reflections about God's creation of you:

How did I see the creative beauty of God as I looked at and thought about myself?

_____

_____

_____

_____

_____

What did I learn about the person and character of God as I reflected on who he made me to be?

_____

_____

_____

_____

_____

How did I feel wonder and awe as I focused on what God has made?

_____

_____

_____

_____

_____

Day 2

Continue learning and meditating on this week's memory verse. Think about how you were made in the image of God and how he wants you to be creative, just as he is.

The heavens declare the glory of God; the skies proclaim the work of his hands.

Psalm 19:1

WHAT I REALLY WANT

God himself draws us close, and we behold him—the author of beauty itself.

We all have desires, but many of them are surface and shallow. Take five minutes to pray and reflect on what you really want in life. What is it that matters most? What do you want to look back on when you're nearing the end of your life and know that you pursued with relentless passion?

Make a list of eight to ten things (in no particular order) that really matter to you. What are the things you want that will last, make a difference, bring meaning to life?

1. _____
2. _____
3. _____
4. _____
5. _____

6. _____

7. _____

8. _____

9. _____

10. _____

Spend a few minutes praying that you will devote your life to seeking the things that matter most. Then look at this list and identify one or two things that are most important to you and attainable in the upcoming weeks or months. Use the space below to write a personal plan to pursue one of these in the upcoming week.

_____

_____

_____

_____

_____

_____

_____

_____

_____

_____

_____

_____

_____

_____

Ask one or two members of your small group to pray for you and check in to see how you're doing as you partner with God in seeking what you really want.

Day 3

As you conclude your learning and meditating on this week's memory verse, pray that you will make meaning as you allow God's creative presence and power to be alive in you.

The heavens declare the glory of God; the skies proclaim the work of his hands.

Psalm 19:1

REVIVE A CALLING

God longs to be with us, inspire us, and renew his world through us.

You have callings and gifts that once burned hot in your heart. You naturally acted on them and found delight in them along the way. But some of these have waned. The flame has flickered or gone out. Take time to reflect on your life and identify one birthright gift that you've put on a back shelf of your life but you need to revive.

Write down and reflect on that gift and what it might accomplish in your life.

What is one step you can take to ignite the flame of this calling in this area of your life?

_____

_____

_____

_____

RECOMMENDED READING

As you reflect on what God is teaching you through this session, you may want to read chapters 13–15 of Rebekah's book *Building a Resilient Life*.

ENDURE TOGETHER

We will all face adversity, pain, loss, and times of struggle in our lives. The best way to grow resilient and stand strong through these times is to find community with God's people, his beloved church, the family of God.

INTRODUCTION

Group leader, read the introduction to the group before showing the video for this session.

The term *ball hog* floats around basketball courts, soccer fields, and a lot of other sporting environments. Have you ever sat on the sidelines and watched a kids' sports event where one child tries to play the game alone? There are, of course, other kids on the court or field, but one overly-aggressive player tries to dominate the other team all by themselves. It rarely goes well. Team sports were made for **teams**, not individuals. When all the players get into the game and work well together, it is a thing of beauty.

If you do a quick Google search on the value of teamwork in the marketplace, health-care settings, educational institutions, or almost any other work environment, you will find seemingly endless articles praising the value of community and partnership. We are truly better when we work together!

When Jesus came to our world and brought his good news to the hungry and broken hearts of humanity, he did ***not*** travel alone. If anyone could have been a solo act and spiritual "ball hog," it was Jesus. He was God in human flesh and the One who spoke all of creation into existence. Instead of traveling alone, Jesus gathered twelve disciples, a larger group of men and women to partner in his ministry, and crowds of people to hear and pass on his message. Jesus saw the eternal value of doing life in community.

When the Holy Spirit was inspiring the words of Scripture, he could have dropped a book from heaven—all neat and tidy. What God did was to speak his truth, tell his story, inspire songs and poetry through real people. Farmers, religious folks, tax collectors, fishermen, and people from every walk of life. The truth of heaven was poured into and through real people in real places with real lives.

We are stronger, better, healthier, and more resilient when we walk in community together. It's the way our God has designed us.

The entire story of Scripture from Genesis to Revelation calls us to community.

TALK ABOUT IT

Share a time when you were striving toward something but felt alone and then God brought a person or community of people alongside you. How did things get better and easier when you pursued the same goal but were no longer alone?

Building a resilient life requires intention to come alongside others to embrace the adversity and enjoy the bounty of community.

TEACHING NOTES
FROM VIDEO SESSION 5

As you watch the teaching segment for this session, use the following outline to record anything that stands out to you.

Doing life together . . . A story of God's people being the church

Waking up . . . Revived one by one and revived in community

Isolation is not God's plan

A community that jumps together

We were made to be in relationship
with God and one another.

Jesus was a model of the need for community

The church . . . Growing resilient together

An unshakable community

Waking up from our slumber

Following Jesus in community

Moving forward together with purpose, meaning, and resilience

God's community . . . We have a mission

We are made to overcome.

We are created to be God's messengers.

Overcome trials and grow stronger.

_____

_____

Move forward together with purpose, meaning, and resilience.

_____

_____

Finding hope and strength in community

_____

_____

––––––––––––––

We are a communal people made by a communal God.

––––––––––––––

GROUP DISCUSSION

1. Can you identify some ways you experienced isolation from people you care about during the pandemic or some other time of struggle? How did this impact your life, relationships, and faith?

_____

We were never meant for isolation.

_____

2. What are some ways you are rediscovering and reclaiming the gift of community? How does connecting deeply with God's people strengthen your life, relationships, and faith?

3. *Group leader, look up and read aloud the following passage or invite a volunteer to do so:* **Acts 2:42–47**.

   What were the things God's people were doing as they connected together as a faith community? How do you see these same things happening in the life of the Christian community you are part of? If you don't see them happening, what can you do to spark a new sense of biblical community in your church?

4. Tell about a time you had a common cause and mission with other followers of Jesus. What did you do, and how did this experience connect your hearts and grow resilience in all of you as a group?

_____

Resilience isn't found in the power of me;
it is found in the power of we.

_____

5. *Group leader, look up and read aloud the following passage or invite a volunteer to do so:* **Matthew 13:31–32**.

God loves to amaze us by doing big things in and through small groups of people. Tell about a time you saw God do something powerful in a small group of believers that you were part of or that you heard about (in another part of the world or in another time in history). Let your hearts be ignited and inspired by the power of God displayed in and through a small group of devoted Christians.

6. *Group leader, look up and read aloud the following passage or invite a volunteer to do so:* **John 17:20–26**.

John 17 contains the longest prayer of Jesus in the pages of Scripture. When we get to verse 20, Jesus has already prayed for the glory of the Father and the unity of his disciples, and now he is praying for those who will one day believe in him through the ministry of the early disciples. He is praying for us! What specific things does the Savior pray for us, and how are we doing in fulfilling this passionate cry of Jesus' heart? What can we do to seek greater unity with God's people and serve others in his name?

7. How can living in authentic community with other believers help us accomplish **one** of these callings that God has placed on his people?

   - To find victory in the battles God has called us to fight

   - To be messengers of God's kingdom and share his good news

   - To serve the broken, forgotten, and marginalized in our communities

   - To face adversity boldly

   - To grow more resilient as we follow our Savior each day of our lives

*God calls us into abundant life, and the only
way to build resilient lives is **together**.*

CLOSING PRAYER

*Spend time in your group praying together. The group leader may pray over the
group or ask for volunteers. Below are some suggested prayer prompts:*

- Thank God that we are in a season where we can connect more freely and experience community with fewer obstacles.

- Pray for creativity in yourself and others as we discover new ways to emulate the ancient model of the church we see described in the book of Acts.

- As you draw near the end of this specific study, ask God to help each member of your group experience the blessing of community in deeper ways and grow more resilient in their life and faith.

- Thank Jesus for being a perfect example of seeking community and strength in the fellowship of God's people.

- Pray that the lessons you've learned and truth you've embraced over these five sessions will stay with you and your group members for a lifetime!

*With God's help, adversity is meant to make us stronger.
Through that Spirit-born strength, we become a living
model of Christ's power to the world around us.*

WRAP-UP

Group leader, read the following wrap-up as you conclude your group session:

This isn't simply the end of a five-session learning experience; it's a launchpad into our future! Let's commit to identify and *name our pain*—this is the starting point of a resilient life. When we identify the lies and false narratives we face, with the help of the Holy Spirit, let's commit to *shift the narrative* and embrace God's truth. When pain, sorrow, and adversity come crashing onto the shores of our lives, let's decide that we won't run for the hills but will instead *embrace adversity* with the wisdom of God and the help of other believers. As we recognize and lament over the meaninglessness in so much of our world, let's decide to *make meaning* as we discover beauty, purpose, and God's vision for our lives. And then as we walk this journey of life with all of its joys and sorrows, let's promise to *endure together* and refuse the folly of isolation.

This is not the end of our voyage of growing resilient; it is just the beginning. May God richly bless each and every one of us as we follow Jesus on this adventure.

_____

Adversity awakens us to what it means to follow Christ.

_____

BETWEEN SESSIONS

Make time in three days of the upcoming week to go deeper into *Building a Resilient Life* by using the resources provided here in your study guide. If you do these exercises slowly and reflectively each day, it should take about 20–30 minutes.

PERSONAL STUDY

ENDURE TOGETHER

Day 1

MEMORY VERSE

Take time to begin learning and meditating on this week's memory verse. As you do, humbly ask yourself if there are any ways you may be contributing to division or disunity in the church. Where you may be falling short, ask for forgiveness and strength to turn from these behaviors.

> *God has put the body [the church] together . . . so that there should be no division in the body [the church], but that its parts should have equal concern for each other. If one part suffers, every part suffers with it; if one part is honored, every part rejoices with it.*
>
> **1 Corinthians 12:24–26**

THREE NEW CONNECTIONS

———————

Being resilient isn't about being a solo hero; it's the wisdom to know you need others before you actually do.

———————

It is possible to be around a small (or large) group of people and still be isolated. Showing up for a church service does not guarantee that you will experience community. Connecting with other people is a decision we must make over and over again.

In the upcoming week, can you make three new connections or go deeper in three existing relationships in God's family? The next time you go to a church service or a gathering of any kind, commit to slowing down, looking around, and identifying three people you don't know (or haven't connected with beyond a smile and a friendly hello). Seek to engage them in a conversation, and be sure to ask these or similar questions once you've said hello and broken the ice:

1. How was your past week? Did anything happen that made it a memorable week?

2. What is one thing you enjoy about being part of this Christian community (gathering/church)?

3. Can you share at least one thing I can pray about for you in the upcoming week?

Write down a few notes for each person you talk with so you can remember what they shared and so you can keep praying for them. If you see them the next week, let them know you've been praying and ask them for an update.

Person 1 Name: _____

Notes and prayer direction …

_____

_____

_____

_____

_____

Person 2 Name: _____

Notes and prayer direction ...

_____

_____

_____

_____

_____

Person 3 Name: _____

Notes and prayer direction ...

_____

_____

_____

_____

_____

Day 2

MEMORY VERSE

Continue learning and meditating on this week's memory verse. Ask God to grow compassion in your heart and develop practices that express concern for others in the church.

God has put the body [the church] together . . . so that there should be no division in the body [the church], but that its parts should have equal concern for each other. If one part suffers, every part suffers with it; if one part is honored, every part rejoices with it.

1 Corinthians 12:24–26

ACTS 2 COMMUNITY

The resilience of a community is not dependent on the size; it's about people who are committed to obeying God together.

Take time to dig into **Acts 2:42–47**. Read the passage three or four times and think about ways to enter into the kind of dynamic and connectional community the believers experienced two thousand years ago.

They devoted themselves to the apostles' teaching and to fellowship, to the breaking of bread and to prayer. Everyone was filled with awe at the many wonders and signs performed by the apostles. All the believers were together and had everything in common. They sold property and possessions to give to anyone who had need. Every day they continued to meet together in the temple courts. They broke bread in their homes and ate together with glad and sincere hearts, praising God and enjoying the favor of all the people. And the Lord added to their number daily those who were being saved.

Write down one or two ideas of ways you can engage in the following:

Ways I can **go deeper into the teachings of the Bible** in the community of God's people:

1. _____
2. _____

Ways I can **share meals and "break bread and eat together"** in the community of God's people:

1. _____
2. _____

Ways I can **pray more** with other believers:

1. _____
2. _____

Ways I can **share what I have and be more generous** with people in my church family and community:

1. _____
2. _____

Ways I can **sing, worship, and praise God** with other believers:

1. _____

2. _____

Ways I can **share the good news of Jesus** in the community of God's people:

1. _____

2. _____

Decide on one specific action to take in the next week from the ideas above—and be sure to do it!

Day 3

As you conclude your time of learning and meditating on this week's memory verse, think of ways to walk with people through their pain and their joy.

*God has put the body [the church] together
. . . so that there should be no division in the
body [the church], but that its parts should
have equal concern for each other. If one
part suffers, every part suffers with it; if one
part is honored, every part rejoices with it.*

1 Corinthians 12:24–26

JOINING JESUS IN PRAYER

_____

Building a resilient life cannot be done alone.

_____

Read through Jesus' prayer in **John 17**. The whole chapter is a prayer. Write down three prayer lessons from the Savior and list them below:

Prayer Lesson 1:

_____

_____

Prayer Lesson 2:

_____

_____

Prayer Lesson 3:

_____

_____

Seek to embed this lesson and practice of prayer into your own prayer times this week.

RECOMMENDED READING

As you reflect on what God is teaching you through this session, you may want to read chapters 16–18 of Rebekah's book *Building a Resilient Life.*

SMALL GROUP LEADER HELPS

If you are reading this, you have likely agreed to lead a group through *Building a Resilient Life*. Thank you! What you have chosen to do is important, and much good fruit can come from studies like this. The rewards of being a leader are different from those of participating, and we hope you find your own walk with Jesus deepened by this experience.

Building a Resilient Life is a five-session study built around video content and small-group interaction. As the group leader, imagine yourself as the host of a dinner party. Your job is to take care of your guests by managing all the behind-the-scenes details so that as your guests arrive, they can focus on each other and on interaction around the topic.

As the group leader, your role is not to answer all the questions or reteach the content—the video, book, and study guide will do most of that work. Your job is to guide the experience and cultivate your small group into a kind of teaching community. This will make it a place for members to process, question, and reflect—not receive more instruction.

There are several elements in this leader's guide that will help you as you structure your study and reflection time, so follow along and take advantage of each one.

BEFORE YOU BEGIN

Before your first meeting, make sure the participants have a copy of this study guide so they can follow along and have their answers written out ahead of time. Alternately, you can hand out the study guides at your first meeting and give the group members some time to look over the material and ask any preliminary questions. During your first meeting, be sure to send a sheet of paper around the room and have the members write down their names, phone numbers, and email addresses so you can keep in touch with them during the week.

Generally, the ideal size for a group is between eight to ten people, which ensures everyone will have enough time to participate in discussions. If you have more people, you might want to break up the main group into smaller subgroups. Encourage those who show up at the first meeting to commit to attending the duration of the study, as this will help the group members get to know each other, create stability for the group, and help you know how to prepare each week.

Each of the sessions begins with an opening illustration, which the leader can read or summarize. The choice of questions that follow serve as an icebreaker to get the group members thinking about the topic at hand. Some people may want to tell a long story in response to one of these questions, but the goal is to keep the answers brief. Ideally, you want everyone in the group to get a chance to answer, so try to keep the responses to a minute or less. If you have talkative group members, say up front that everyone needs to limit his or her answer to one minute.

Give the group members a chance to answer, but tell them to feel free to pass if they wish. With the rest of the study, it's generally not a good idea to have everyone answer every question—a free-flowing discussion is more desirable. But with the opening icebreaker questions, you can go around the circle. Encourage shy people to share, but don't force them.

Before your first meeting, let the group members know that each session contains three days' worth of Bible study and reflection materials that they can complete during the week. While this is an optional exercise, it will help the members cement the concepts presented during the group study time and encourage them to spend additional time in God's Word on their own. Also invite them to bring any questions and insights they uncovered while reading to your next meeting, especially if they had a breakthrough moment or if they didn't understand something.

WEEKLY PREPARATION

As the leader, there are a few things you should do to prepare for each meeting:

- *Read through the session.* This will help you to become familiar with the content and know how to structure the discussion times.

- *Decide which questions you definitely want to discuss.* Based on the amount and length of group discussion, you may not be able to get through all the questions, so choose four to five questions that you definitely want to cover.

- *Be familiar with the questions you want to discuss.* When the group meets, you'll be watching the clock, so you want to make sure you are familiar with the questions you have selected. In this way, you'll ensure you have the material more deeply in your mind than your group members.

- *Pray for your group.* Pray for your group members throughout the week and ask God to lead them as they study his Word.

- *Bring extra supplies to your meeting.* The members should bring their own pens for writing notes, but it's a good idea to have extras available for those who forget. You may also want to bring paper and additional Bibles.

Note that in many cases there will be no one "right" answer to the question. Answers will vary, especially when the group members are being asked to share their personal experiences.

STRUCTURING THE DISCUSSION TIME

You will need to determine with your group how long you want to meet each week so you can plan your time accordingly. Generally, most groups like to meet for either sixty minutes or ninety minutes, so you could use one of the following schedules:

SECTION	60 minutes	90 minutes
Introduction (members arrive and get settled; leader reads or summarizes introduction)	5 minutes	10 minutes
Talk About It (discuss one of the two opening questions for the session)	10 minutes	15 minutes
Video Notes (watch the teaching material together and take notes)	15 minutes	15 minutes
Group Discussion (discuss the Bible study questions you selected ahead of time)	25 minutes	40 minutes
Closing Prayer (pray together as a group and dismiss)	5 minutes	10 minutes

As the group leader, it is up to you to keep track of the time and keep things moving along according to your schedule. You might want to set a timer for each segment so both you and the group members know when your time is up. (Note that there are some good phone apps for timers that play a gentle chime or other pleasant sound instead of a disruptive noise.)

Don't be concerned if the group members are quiet or slow to share. People are often quiet when they are pulling together their ideas, and this might be a new experience for them. Just ask a question and let it hang in the air until someone shares. You can then say, "Thank you. What about others? What came to you when you watched that portion of the video?"

GROUP DYNAMICS

Leading a group through *Building a Resilient Life* will prove to be highly rewarding both to you and your group members. However, this doesn't mean you will not encounter any challenges along the way! Discussions can get off track. Group members may not be sensitive to the needs and ideas of others. Some might worry they will be expected to talk about matters that make them feel awkward. Others may express comments that result in disagreements. To help ease this strain on you and the group, consider the following ground rules:

- When someone raises a question or comment that is off the main topic, suggest you deal with it another time, or, if you feel led to go in that direction, let the group know you will be spending some time discussing it.

- If someone asks a question you don't know how to answer, admit it and move on. At your discretion, feel free to invite group members to comment on questions that call for personal experience.

- If you find one or two people are dominating the discussion time, direct a few questions to others in the group. Outside the main group time, ask the more dominating members to help you draw out the quieter ones. Work to make them a part of the solution instead of the problem.

When a disagreement occurs, encourage the group members to process the matter in love. Encourage those on opposite sides to restate what they heard the other side say about the matter, and then invite each side to evaluate if that perception is accurate. Lead the group in examining other Scriptures related to the topic and look for common ground.

When any of these issues arise, encourage your group members to follow these words from the Bible: "Love one another" (John 13:34); "If it is possible, as far as it depends on you, live at peace with everyone" (Romans 12:18); and "Be quick to listen, slow to speak and slow to become angry" (James 1:19). This will make your group time more rewarding and beneficial for everyone who attends.

ABOUT THE AUTHOR

Rebekah Lyons is a national speaker, host of the *Rhythms for Life* podcast, and bestselling author of *Rhythms of Renewal, You Are Free,* and *Freefall to Fly.* An old soul with a contemporary, honest voice, Rebekah reveals her own battles to overcome anxiety and depression, and invites others to discover and boldly pursue their God-given purpose. Alongside her husband, Gabe, Rebekah finds joy in raising four children, two of whom have Down syndrome. Her work has been featured on *The TODAY Show, Good Morning America,* CNN, FOX News, *Publishers Weekly* Starred Reviews, and more.

RHYTHMS FOR LIFE PODCAST

Join Rebekah & Gabe for conversations with experts and access free resources to build resilience in your emotional, spiritual and relational health.

RebekahLyons.com/Free

RHYTHMS OF RENEWAL

Trading Stress and Anxiety for a Life of Peace and Purpose

DISCOVER HOW TO:

- Take charge of your emotional health & invite others to do the same.
- Overcome anxiety with daily habits that strengthen you mentally.
- Find joy through restored relationships in your family & community.
- Walk in confidence with the unique gifts you have to offer the world.

Available in stores and online!

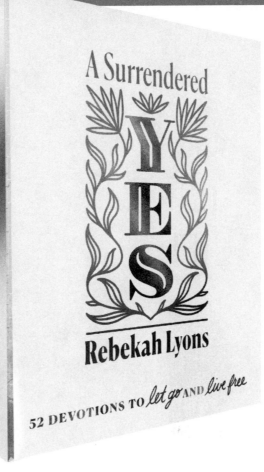

RESOURCES

JOIN THE WELLNESS JOURNEY
Continue to build your resilience with the following:

FREE RESOURCES AT WWW.REBEKAHLYONS.COM

Tech Detox Guide: https://rebekahlyons.com/techdetox

30 Verses for Anxiety: https://rebekahlyons.com/anxiety

Take Inventory Guide: https://rebekahlyons.com/takeinventory

Fighting Fear Guide: https://rebekahlyons.com/fightingfear

Strength & Dignity Study: https://www.rebekahlyons.com/strength

10 Tips for Mental Health: https://rebekahlyons.com/mentalhealth

A Three-Week Study on Confidence: https://www.rebekahlyons.com/confidence

A Ten-Day Video Study on Rest: https://rebekahlyons.com/rest

A Six-Week Video Study on Freedom: https://rebekahlyons.com/freedom

Healthiest Rhythm Quiz: https://rebekahlyons.com/quiz

Weekly Rhythm Guide: https://www.rebekahlyons.com/rhythmguide

3 Ways to Overcome Loneliness Webinar: https://rebekahlyons.com/replay

Live Free Conversation Guide: https://rebekahlyons.com/livefree

Emotional Health Series: https://rebekahlyons.com/emotionalhealth

CHAPTER DOWNLOADS

Embracing Your Calling: https://rebekahlyons.com/calling

Take a Walk: https://rebekahlyons.com/takeawalk

Morning Routine: https://rebekahlyons.com/morningroutine

Free to Grieve: https://rebekahlyons.com/grief

Free to Rest: https://rebekahlyons.com/free-to-rest

Permission to Play: https://rebekahlyons.com/play

RETREATS: RebekahLyons.com/retreats

Rhythms Retreat: https://rebekahlyons.com/rhythmsretreat

Emotional Health Retreat: https://rebekahlyons.com/ehretreat

Chrystal Evans Hurst

Lisa Whittle

Wendy Blight

Sandra Richter

Lysa TerKeurst

Karen Ehman

Lynn Cowell

Jada Edwards

Ruth Chou Simons

Jennie Allen

Christine Caine

Shannon Bream

Ann Voskamp

Lisa Harper

Rebekah Lyons

Lori Wilhite

Anne Graham Lotz

Megan Marshman

Margaret Feinberg

From the Publisher

GREAT STUDIES

ARE EVEN BETTER WHEN THEY'RE SHARED!

Help others find this study:

- Post a review at your favorite online bookseller.

- Post a picture on a social media account and share why you enjoyed it.

- Send a note to a friend who would also love it—or, better yet, go through it with them.

Thanks for helping others grow their faith!